Copyrights © 2025 Sierra Ponce
All rights reserved. No part of this publication may be reproduced, distributed, or transmitted in any form or by any means without the prior written permission of the author.

DEDICATION

For Nova Rose—This book is for you.
For your strong will, boundless curiosity,
and the magic you bring into the world.
May you always dare to try new things
and see them through till the end.

ACKNOWLEDGMENTS

Creating this book has been a journey filled with wonder and the excitement of creating something new. I want to thank my best friend, Trevor, for believing in my vision and inspiring me to bring this story to life. To my parents, thank you for your endless love and encouragement. Your support means everything to me. To the children who will read this book— you are the reason I write. May you always believe that you are capable of creating anything you dream of if you're willing to try. Lastly, to Albert Wright, thank you for inspiring me to write. This book is as much yours as it is mine.

ABOUT THE AUTHOR

Sierra Rayne Ponce has always loved stories—reading them, imagining them, and now sharing them with young readers. Inspired by Albert Wright during a training session on fostering children's confidence through literacy, and by the daycare classroom where she works, Sierra writes stories that celebrate the joy of learning and growing up. When not writing, Sierra enjoys painting and spending time with her family. She lives in Fredericksburg, TX, with her best friend and child. This is Sierra's first children's book, and she hopes it will inspire readers to try something new and have the confidence to share their efforts with others, no matter what the outcome looks like.

Lucky the bunny comes to class with mama. He was scared, now comes the drama.

Kicking, squirming,
screaming too.
Good thing my teacher
knows what to do

"Good morning!" she says with love, then wraps me up in a great big hug.
"Big feelings are okay, we're going to have a fantastic day!"

Mama leaves with a
soft goodbye.
My teacher says,
"It's okay to cry."
My friends come running,
toys in hand.
Drums, miracas,
a whole great band!

Playing, laughing,
my friends all call me,
but I'm still sad.

I just want mommy.

I go to the Library to take a rest.

My teacher says,

"Take a belly breath."

"First, smell the flower,
now blow out the candle"
That's something
I think I can handle.
In and out each
breath calms me down.
Wow, Im so glad that
my teachers around!

I'm feeling much better,
I'm ready to play!
It WILL be a fantastic day!
My friends are all here,
and these toys are so cool!
I am so lucky to go to preschool

www.ingramcontent.com/pod-product-compliance
Lightning Source LLC
LaVergne TN
LVHW072115060526
838201LV00011B/242